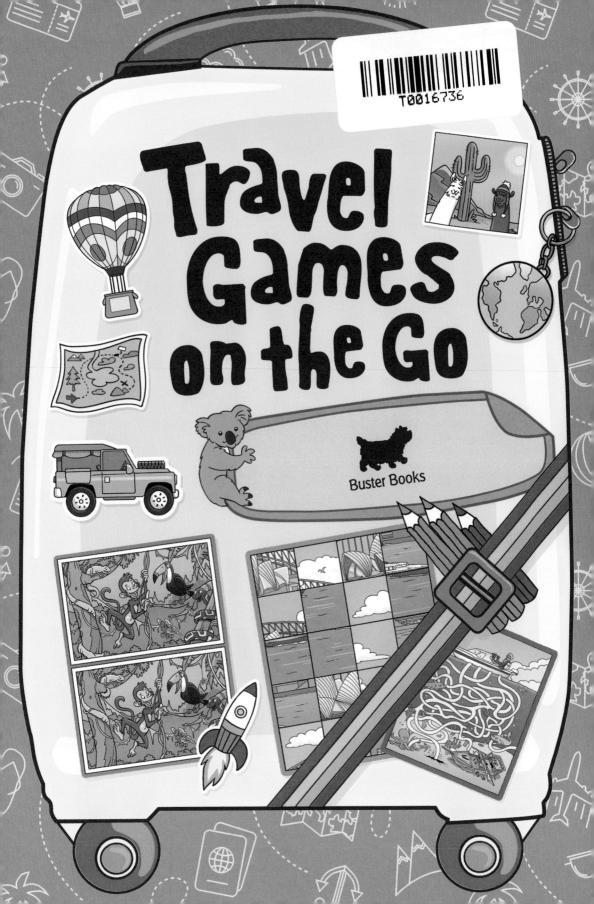

Travel Games on the Go

Buster Books

T0016736

**ILLUSTRATED BY
JORGE SANTILLAN**

**EDITED BY
EMMA TAYLOR**

**DESIGNED BY
JADE MOORE**

**COVER DESIGN BY
JAKE DA'COSTA & JADE MOORE**

**ADDITIONAL ARTWORK BY
ANDY ROWLAND & EMILY GOLDEN TWOMEY**

First published in Great Britain in 2023 by Buster Books,
an imprint of Michael O'Mara Books Limited,
9 Lion Yard, Tremadoc Road, London SW4 7NQ

 www.mombooks.com/buster   Buster Books @BusterBooks @buster_books

A CIP catalogue record for this book is available from the British Library.

ISBN: 978-1-78055-714-4

1 3 5 7 9 10 8 6 4 2

This book was printed in November 2022 by Leo Paper Products Ltd,
Heshan Astros Printing Limited, Xuantan Temple Industrial Zone,
Gulao Town, Heshan City, Guangdong Province, China.

HOW TO USE THIS BOOK

This book is packed full of puzzles to make any journey fly by. From mind-bending mazes and dot-to-dots to spot-the-difference games and sudoku puzzles, your travels will be filled with all kinds of fun.

Follow the instructions on each page and, once a puzzle is completed, check your answers at the back of the book. You can work through it from the beginning or dip in and out.

Whether you're waiting for a plane or train, or relaxing on your holidays, grab your pens and pencils and get going!

MONKEY MAZE

Guide the monkey through the trees to reach the rainforest floor. You can go over and under branches, but you can't pass the obstacles in the way.

4

MASTER BUILDER

This is a picture of the Statue of Liberty in New York, the United States of America. Using the squares in the grid below, can you copy it?

SUITCASE SILHOUETTES

Write each suitcase's number beneath the silhouette that matches it.

1

2

3

4

5

6

7

8

9

10

11

12

A.............

B.............

C.............

D.............

E.............

F.............

G.............

H.............

I.............

J.............

K.............

L.............

6

SPOT THE DIFFERENCE

Can you find the six differences between these two island scenes?

FLAG FUN

Can you unscramble the name of each country below?
The flag for each country has been given as a clue to help you.

NYGREMA

ANCAAD

ILAUTARSA

NCIHA

UOTHS FRAIAC

INAGRNETA

MATCHING PAIRS

Draw a line to match each ice cream to its twin.

SEASHELL SUDOKU

Fill in the large grid with the six types of seashell below. Each row, column and six-square block must contain one of each shell.

Look at the example on the right. Now try it for yourself below.

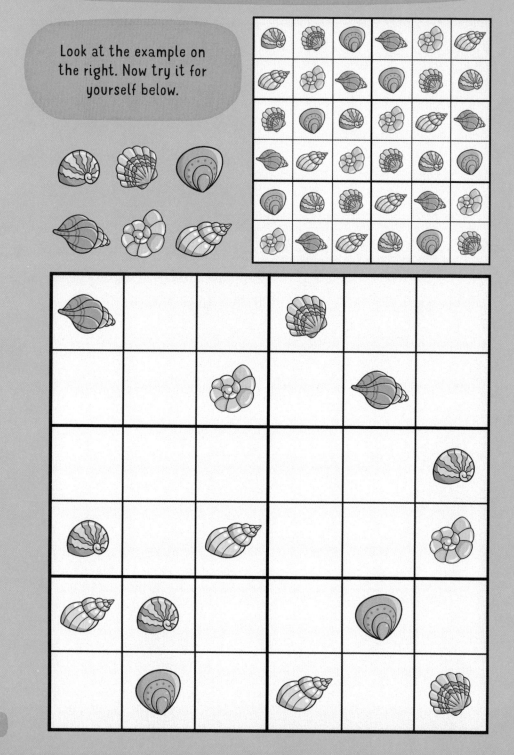

SUPER SOUVENIRS

This shop sells souvenirs. Can you find the odd one out in each row?

JIGSAW PUZZLE

Circle the three pieces that will finish this jigsaw puzzle.

AIRPORT WORDSEARCH

Can you solve this airport-themed wordsearch? The words you need to search for are listed on the seats below.

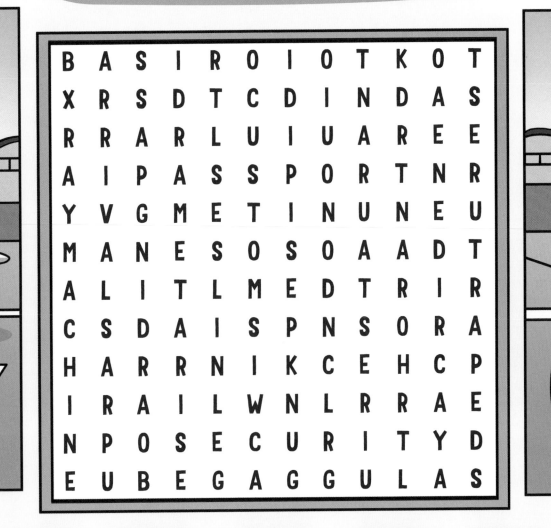

```
B A S I R O I O T K O T
X R S D T C D I N D A S
R R A R L U I U A R E E
A I P A S S P O R T N R
Y V G M E T I N U N E U
M A N E S O S O A A D T
A L I T L M E D T R I R
C S D A I S P N S O R A
H A R R N I K C E H C P
I R A I L W N L R R A E
N P O S E C U R I T Y D
E U B E G A G G U L A S
```

Arrivals
Boarding pass
Check-in
Customs
Departures
Luggage
Passport
Restaurant
Security
X-ray machine

AIRCRAFT ANTICS

How many aircraft outlines can you count below?

ANSWER: ....

NUMBER PYRAMIDS

Can you solve these number pyramids?
Each section should contain a number that is
equal to the sum of the two blocks below it.

22   38

9   13   21

13

6   7   8

FESTIVAL FUN

How many new words can you make using the ten letters of the word below? Add up the total score of all of your words – a two letter word scores two points, a three letter word scores three points, and so on. Use the empty space to write down the new words.

FAIRGROUND

LEFT LUGGAGE

Your family are going on holiday, but your luggage is too heavy for the plane! You can take 150 kilograms of luggage exactly. Can you work out which bag to leave behind?

CAMPSITE CHALLENGE

There are all kinds of objects on this campsite, from a barbecue to a burning log fire. Can you spot six items that are out of place?

MEMORY CHALLENGE

Study the items on this page for one minute. Try to remember as many of them as you can. Then, turn the page and see if you can work out which ones are missing.

MEMORY CHALLENGE

Can you work out which items are missing?

ANSWER:

....

....

....

TRAVEL GUIDE

LLAMA DRAMA

Can you move just three of these llamas so that
the triangle they make points down instead of up?

HOW TO DRAW A PLANE

Follow these simple steps to draw your very own plane below.

1) Draw the body of the plane.

2) Draw windows and a door.

3) Draw the wings and a tail.

4) Now add the final details.

LET IT SNOW

Draw a line from the skier to the finish line as fast as you can without coming off the track. Next, have a go with the opposite hand, and then try it with your eyes closed. How close to the finish line do you end up?

FINISH

COORDINATE CHALLENGE

You're visiting a holiday park. Can you find all of the attractions?
Work out the coordinates for each one listed below.

1. Bicycle hire .... 2. Carousel .... 3. Playground ....
4. Ice-cream truck .... 5. Café ....

24

TRAVEL TRIVIA

Test your knowledge of the world with this fun, fact-filled quiz.
If you find some of the questions tricky, try to make a logical guess.
The answers can be found at the back of the book.

1. The Great Pyramid of Giza is found in which country?
a) China   b) Egypt   c) New Zealand

2. The Channel Tunnel links which two European countries?
a) The United Kingdom and France   b) Denmark and Norway
c) The United Kingdom and Ireland

3. What is the smallest country in the world?
a) Luxembourg   b) Vatican City   c) Wales

4. Which Italian city is famous for its many canals?
a) Milan   b) Naples   c) Venice

5. Which desert covers much of northern Africa?
a) Gobi   b) Sahara   c) Antarctic

6. What is the biggest country in the world?
a) Russia   b) China   c) Canada

7. What is the capital city of Japan?
a) Beijing   b) Tokyo   c) Mumbai

8. Which country has the biggest population?
a) USA   b) China   c) Australia

SUPER SANDCASTLES

Five children have taken part in a sandcastle building competition.
The judges have marked their castles out of 40. Use the clues
below to find out how many points each of them scored.
Who won the competition?

Jared's sandcastle scored $\frac{2}{5}$ of the possible points.

Tom's sandcastle scored 36.

Lucy scored 75% of the possible 40 points.

Alex scored half as many points as Tom.

Esther scored 4 more points than Lucy.

WINNER: ....

TRAVEL INVENTIONS

Can you label these inventions from 1 to 6 in the order they were first invented? Use 1 for the earliest.

ESCALATOR

ELECTRONIC ROOM KEY

MAGNETIC COMPASS

HELICOPTER

THE FIRST CAMERA

CRUISE SHIP

DOT TO DOT

Complete these two dot-to-dot puzzles and add some colour to bring this awesome aerial scene to life.

BEACH BARGAINS

You're at the beach in Florida, USA. Can you calculate how much it would cost to buy each of the following items?

1. Two ice creams and a beach ball $ ....

2. Three deck chairs $ ....

3. A pair of flippers and a beach towel $ ....

4. A bucket and spade and a pair of sunglasses $ ....

5. A hat and two surfboards $ ....

CURRENCY CHAOS

Draw a line to match these currencies to their country.
The first one has been done for you to help you get started.

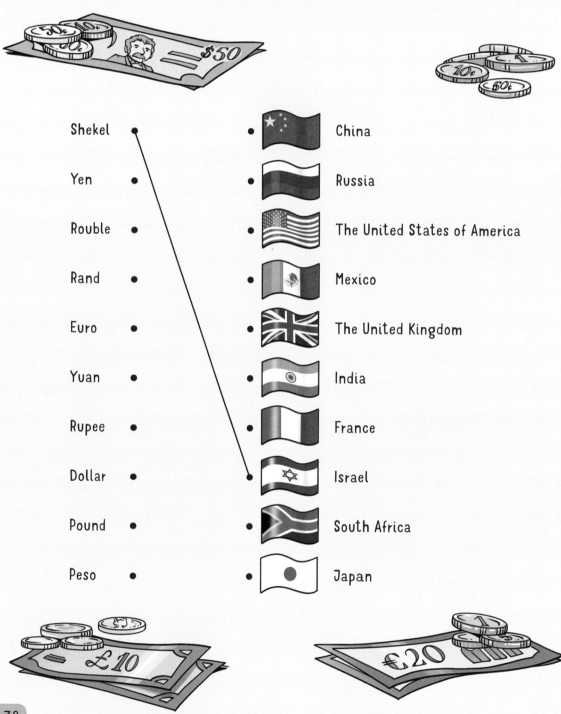

Shekel

Yen

Rouble

Rand

Euro

Yuan

Rupee

Dollar

Pound

Peso

China

Russia

The United States of America

Mexico

The United Kingdom

India

France

Israel

South Africa

Japan

MATCHING PAIRS

Draw a line to match each shoe with its identical partner.
Can you work out which shoe is not part of a matching pair?

KOALA COUNT

Colour four of the koalas in red. Colour 50% of the koalas left blank in purple. Colour 25% of the remaining koalas in blue. How many koalas are left uncoloured?

TREASURE HUNT

Guide the pirate ship through the water to reach
the treasure chest on Skull Island.

SKULL
ISLAND

AWESOME ADVENTURE

Imagine you've been on a safari adventure to South Africa
and the local newspaper wants to interview you.
Answer the questions below to share your experience.

DAILY NEWS

Why did you want to go on safari?

_____

_____

_____

_____

What was your favourite animal and why?

_____

_____

_____

_____

Tell us something amazing or funny that happened during the trip.

_____

_____

_____

_____

UP, UP AND AWAY

Each of these hot-air balloons has a different number on it.
Can you work out which balloons add up to the totals below?

A) 98 = ...

B) 152 = ...

C) 211 = ...

5

199

54

50

48

7

DOT TO DOT

Join up the dots and add some colour to bring
this beautiful beach scene to life.

ODD ONE OUT

The objects below can be divided into four groups of three things that have something in common. Circle the object that doesn't belong to any of the groups.

LILY-PAD LEAP

Guide the frogs at the bottom of the page to the lily pads at the top of the page by only jumping on stones that contain multiples of three.

TRAVEL CHALLENGE

Using the clocks below, work out which journey took the shortest amount of time. Was it the train, plane, campervan, boat or helicopter?

DEPARTURE

ARRIVAL

ANSWER: ....

DESIGN YOUR OWN PASSPORT

Use the template below to design your own passport.
Draw stamps for the places you'd like to visit
one day and don't forget to add a self-portrait.

PASSPORT

NAME:

DATE OF BIRTH:

PLACE OF BIRTH:

CAMPING CODES

Use the table below and the clues to crack these codes and work out some of the fun things you might like to do on a camping trip.

If you fancy something sweet you might like to:
2 6 10 8 2   12 10 14 8 16 12 10 18 18 6 20 8

....

When it gets late in the evening you might want to tell:
22 16 6 8 2   8 2 6 14 24 26 8

....

If you get cold you might light a:
28 10 12 30 32 24 14 26

....

If you want to play a game you might go on a:
8 28 10 34 26 36 22 26 14   16 38 36 2

....

When it gets dark you might like to:
8 2 10 14 22 10 40 26

....

2	4	6	8	10	12	14	16	18	20	22	24	26	28	30	32	34	36	38	40
T	M	O	S	A	M	R	H	L	W	G	I	E	C	P	F	V	N	U	Z

COLOUR BY NUMBERS

Follow the colour key to bring this ice-cream truck to life.

1 = brown   2 = red   3 = yellow   4 = pink   5= blue   6 = green

CONTINENT CONUNDRUM

Using your knowledge of the world, can you work out which country is in which continent? Write a number in the pink box next to each country to show which continent it is in. Use the map at the bottom of the page to help you.

CONTINENTS:

1. Africa   2. Antarctica   3. Asia   4. Europe
5. North America   6. Australia and Oceania   7. South America

COUNTRIES:

Argentina		Italy	
Australia		Japan	
Canada		Mexico	
China		New Zealand	
France		The United Kingdom	
India		The United States of America	

MONUMENT MASTERPIECE

Draw in the other half of this famous French symmetrical monument. Do you know what it is called?

ANSWER: ....

TIMELINE CHALLENGE

Can you label these six events in the order they happened?
Use 1 for the earliest and 6 for the latest.

Christopher Columbus sails
to the Americas.

Neil Armstrong lands
on the Moon.

The Wright brothers invent
the first successful aeroplane.

Edmund Hillary and Tenzing Norgay
successfully climb Mount Everest.

Roald Amundsen reaches
the South Pole.

Francis Drake sails
around the world.

CODE BREAKER

The picture below can be rearranged to reveal
a famous landmark. Can you work out what the famous
landmark is and which country it is in?

Write your answer here: ....

EPIC EXPEDITION

Draw a line to help the hiker reach the bottom of the mountain.
You can't pass the snakes and other obstacles that are in the way.

FINISH

WATER WORLD

Can you spot the six differences between these two water park scenes?

FOODS OF THE WORLD

Can you solve this food-related wordsearch?
The foods you need to search for are listed
at the bottom of the page.

```
E  K  A  I  R  S  I  O  Y  K  O  S
A  N  I  D  T  P  D  I  R  D  U  M
R  O  A  M  L  A  I  U  U  S  E  R
L  W  A  A  C  G  Z  L  H  N  N  M
P  R  O  M  N  H  I  I  T  H  E  L
N  E  I  E  A  E  I  O  A  O  D  P
L  U  R  T  C  T  E  G  W  T  I  A
O  G  O  A  H  T  G  N  E  D  R  E
V  A  G  R  O  I  I  O  E  O  D  L
E  R  A  I  S  W  N  L  P  G  A  L
R  P  A  R  M  O  U  S  S  A  K  A
P  R  E  T  Z  E  L  T  H  C  A  S
```

Spaghetti
Paella
Hot dog

Moussaka
Haggis
Sushi
Pretzel

Kimchi
Nachos
Naan

SPEEDY SILHOUETTES

Write each car's number beneath the silhouette that matches it.

1

2

3

4

5

6

7

8

9

10

11

12

A............

B............

C............

D............

E............

F............

G............

H............

I............

J............

K............

L............

TRUE OR FALSE?

Read the ten statements below. Write a 'T' in the box
if you think it's true, or an 'F' if you think it's false.
The answers can be found at the back of the book.

1. The Loch Ness monster is believed to live in Germany.

2. The Bermuda Triangle is located in the Indian Ocean.

3. In total, the Great Wall of China is over 10,000 kilometres (6,200 miles) long.

4. Gladiator fights were once held at Stonehenge.

5. The Statue of Liberty is one of the Seven Wonders of the World.

6. When it's summer in the United Kingdom, it's winter in Australia.

7. Around 70% of the Earth's surface is covered by land.

8. The Golden Gate Bridge is located in the American city of San Francisco.

9. Rainforests cover less than 3% of the planet.

10. The Eiffel Tower in Paris, France, was once painted yellow.

MEMORY SQUARES

Study this page for one minute. Try to remember which pictures are in which squares. Then, turn to the next page and see if you can fill in the blanks correctly.

MEMORY SQUARES

Turn to page 53 to find out how to play this game.

MATCHING PAIRS

Draw a line to match each surfboard to its twin.

TRAVEL BINGO

Your challenge is to spot all of the things shown below while you're out and about. Cross each one off once you've seen it.

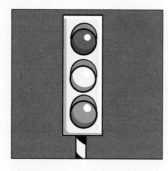

NUMBER PYRAMIDS

Can you solve these number pyramids?
Each square should contain a number that is equal
to the sum of the two blocks below it.

Pyramid 1:
- Top: (blank)
- 25
- 12, (blank), 16

Pyramid 2:
- 239
- (blank), (blank)
- 52, (blank), 67
- (blank), 24, (blank), 31

PACKING JUMBLE

The items of clothing below have been jumbled up. Can you count how many different pieces of clothing there are?

ANSWER: ....

PAIR THEM UP

Draw lines to connect each pair of identical items together. The lines must not cross or touch each other, and only one line is allowed in each grid square. You cannot use diagonal lines.

Look at the example on the right.

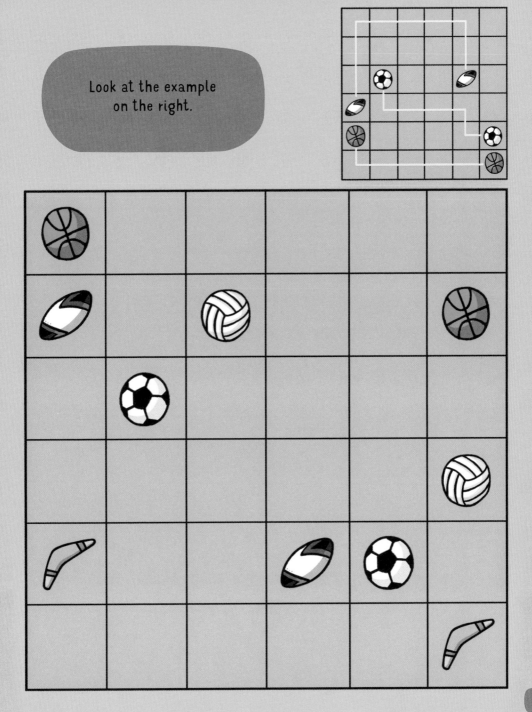

SPOT THE DIFFERENCE

Can you find the six differences between these two underwater scenes?

HOW TO DRAW A LLAMA

Follow these steps to draw your own llama below.

1) Draw the body of the llama.

2) Add some legs.

3) Draw on its head and some feet.

4) Now add the final touches.

WORD MAKER

How many new words can you make using the ten letters of the word below? Write them in the spaces below and then add up the total score of all of your words – a two-letter word scores two points, a three-letter word scores three points, and so on. Then, bring the scene to life with colour.

RAINFOREST

BIRD WATCH

Circle the birds that have a matching pair.

How many birds do not have a pair?   ANSWER: ....

TAXI TIME

Draw a line from the taxi at the airport to the hotel as fast as you can without coming off the road. Next, have a go with the opposite hand, and then try it with your eyes closed. Where do you end up?

HOTEL

JIGSAW JUMBLE

Can you fit all of these jigsaw pieces together in your head and work out what is in the picture? Write your answer in the space below.

ANSWER: ....

TOURIST TRIVIA

Do you know which countries these famous landmarks are in? Write your answers on the dotted lines.

The Sydney Opera House

....

The Statue of Liberty

....

Stonehenge

....

The Colosseum

....

The Eiffel Tower

The Pyramids of Giza

....

The Parthenon

The Taj Mahal

....

PAIR THEM UP

Draw lines to connect each pair of identical fruits together. The lines must not cross or touch each other, and only one line is allowed in each grid square. You cannot use diagonal lines.

Look at the example on the right.

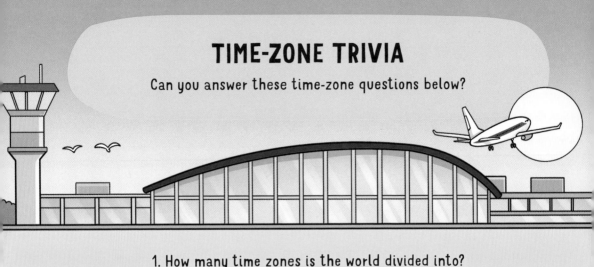

TIME-ZONE TRIVIA

Can you answer these time-zone questions below?

1. How many time zones is the world divided into?

a) 24   b) 12   c) 18

2. Which of these countries has more than one time zone?

a) Portugal   b) Canada   b) New Zealand

3. When it is daytime in the United Kingdom, why is it night-time in Australia?

a) They are on opposite sides of the Earth.

b) They have different seasons.

c) They are different distances from the Sun.

4. London is six hours ahead of Mexico.
When it's 3 pm in London, what time is it in Mexico?

a) 12 pm   b) 9 am   c) 9 pm

5. It's 2 pm in Barcelona. New York is six hours behind, Mumbai is four hours ahead and Cairo is one hour ahead. Can you write the name of the city under the digital clock displaying the correct time?

15:00   **08:00**   **18:00**

PICTURE SUDOKU

Fill in the large grid with these six different insects. Each row, column and six-square block must contain one of each.

Look at the example on the right. Now try it for yourself below.

TREASURE TROVE FIX

You've uncovered a hidden treasure chest on a desert island, but some of the treasure has broken in half. Can you work out which pieces go together so that you can fix them? There are two correct halves for each piece of treasure. Draw a line between the pieces that go together.

BALLOON CHAOS

Jasmine, Aaron, Noah, Emily and Mohammed have all brought their balloons to the park. One of their balloons has come loose from its thread. Can you work out whose balloon is about to fly away?

Jasmine   Aaron   Noah   Emily   Mohammed

ANSWER: ....

TRANSPORT SUDOKU

Fill in the grid with these six types of vehicle. Each row, column and six-square block must contain one of each.

Look at the example on the right. Now try it for yourself below.

ODD ONE OUT

All of these hot-air balloons look identical, but three are different. Can you circle the odd ones out?

SAFARI SURPRISE

Follow the trails to work out which safari truck is heading for which type of animal. Write the letter of the truck in the empty box next to each animal.

TRANSPORT WORDSEARCH

Can you solve this transport-themed wordsearch?
The words are listed at the bottom of the page.

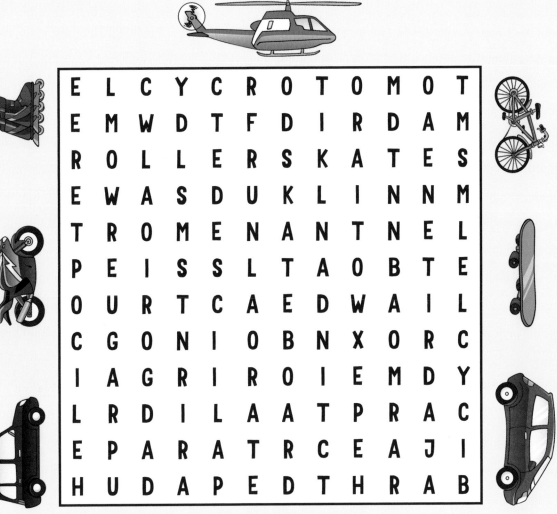

```
E L C Y C R O T O M O T
E M W D T F D I R D A M
R O L L E R S K A T E S
E W A S D U K L I N N M
T R O M E N A N T N E L
P E I S S L T A O B T E
O U R T C A E D W A I L
C G O N I O B N X O R C
I A G R I R O I E M D Y
L R D I L A A T P R A C
E P A R A T R C E A J I
H U D A P E D T H R A B
```

Scooter
Taxi
Bicycle

Train
Helicopter
Skateboard
Rollerskates

Boat
Motorcycle
Car

PENGUIN PARADE

Can you spot the ten penguins hidden in this crowded scene?

MARKET MAYHEM

Study this busy market scene. How many of each of the items on the checklist opposite can you spot? Write the number in the boxes then add up all of your answers. Does your total match the number in the box?

Bicycles

Red caps

Birds

Cats

Guitars

Vases
for sale

Sun
umbrellas

Rugs
for sale

Total = 20

COLOUR BY NUMBERS

Follow the colour key underneath the picture to
bring this serene surf scene to life.

1 = orange   2 = pink   3 = red   4 = green

5= light blue   6 = dark blue   7 = yellow   8 = brown

PLAYGROUND PUZZLE

Can you draw three straight lines to divide this playground into four separate areas? Each area must contain one seesaw, one slide and one set of swings.

MASTER BUILDER

This is a picture of the Golden Gate Bridge in San Francisco, California. Using the squares in the grid below, can you copy it?

ODD ONE OUT

These sea turtles look identical but three are different.
Can you circle the odd ones out?

MAGIC MIRROR CHALLENGE

Can you circle the correct mirror image reflection for each picture?

85

DEEP-SEA DIVE

Can you work out which route the scuba diver should take through the water to reach the sunken ship? Be careful as you can't pass the sharks that are in the way.

A B C D

TRAVEL BINGO

Your challenge is to spot all of the things shown below while you're out and about. Cross each one off once you've seen it.

SPOT THE DIFFERENCE

Can you find the six differences between these two jungle scenes?

HOW TO DRAW A ROCKET

Follow these steps to draw your own rocket in the space below.

1) Draw the body of the rocket.

2) Add a window at the top.

3) Add some more detail.

4) Now add the final touches.

ANSWERS

MONKEY MAZE
Page 4

SUITCASE SILHOUETTES
Page 6

A6	B11	C4	D10
E9	F1	G12	H7
I8	J2	K3	L5

SPOT THE DIFFERENCE
Page 7

FLAG FUN
Page 8
NYGREMA = Germany
ANCAAD = Canada
ILAUTARSA = Australia
NCIHA = China
UOTHS FRAIAC = South Africa
INAGRNETA = Argentina

MATCHING PAIRS
Page 9

SEASHELL SUDOKU
Page 10

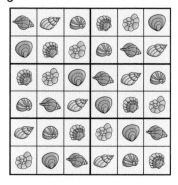

SUPER SOUVENIRS
Page 11

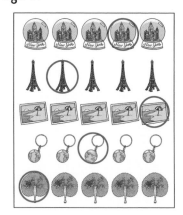

JIGSAW PUZZLE
Page 12

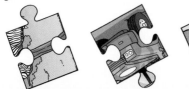

AIRPORT WORDSEARCH
Page 13

AIRCRAFT ANTICS
Page 14
There are 14 aircraft outlines.

NUMBER PYRAMIDS
Page 15

LEFT LUGGAGE
Page 17

CAMPSITE CHALLENGE
Page 18

MEMORY CHALLENGE
Page 20
The missing items are the mobile
phone, passport, water bottle and pen.

LLAMA DRAMA
Page 21

COORDINATE CHALLENGE
Page 24

1. 4C	3. 6B	5. 5F
2. 5D	4. 1B	

TRAVEL TRIVIA
Page 25

1. b	4. c	7. b
2. a	5. b	8. b
3. b	6. a	

SUPER SANDCASTLES
Page 26
The winner is Tom.

TRAVEL INVENTIONS
Page 27
1. Magnetic compass
2. The first camera
3. Escalator
4. Cruise ship
5. Helicopter
6. Electronic room key

BEACH BARGAINS
Page 29
1. $6.50   3. $10   5. $31.50
2. $34.50   4. $8.20

CURRENCY CHAOS
Page 30
Shekel = Israel
Yen = Japan
Rouble = Russia
Rand = South Africa
Euro = France
Yuan = China
Rupee = India
Dollar = The United States of America
Pound = The United Kingdom
Peso = Mexico

MATCHING PAIRS
Page 31

KOALA COUNT
Page 32
6 koalas should be left uncoloured.

TREASURE HUNT
Page 33

UP, UP AND AWAY
Page 35
A) 98 = 48 + 50
B) 152 = 48 + 50 + 54
C) 211 = 5 + 7 + 199

ODD ONE OUT
Page 38

LILY-PAD LEAP
Page 39

TRAVEL CHALLENGE

Page 40

The boat took the shortest amount of time.

CAMPING CODES

Page 42

1. Toast marshmallows
2. Ghost stories
3. Campfire
4. Scavenger hunt
5. Stargaze

CONTINENT CONUNDRUM

Page 44

Argentina = 7
Australia = 6
Canada = 5
China = 3
France = 4
India = 3
Italy = 4
Japan = 3
Mexico = 7
New Zealand = 6
The United Kingdom = 4
The United States of America = 5

TIMELINE CHALLENGE

Page 46

1. Christopher Columbus sails to the Americas.
2. Francis Drake sails around the world.
3. The Wright brothers invent the first successful aeroplane.
4. Roald Amundsen reaches the South Pole.
5. Edmund Hillary and Tenzing Norgay successfully climb Mount Everest.
6. Neil Armstrong lands on the Moon.

CODE BREAKER

Page 47

The Sydney Opera House, Australia

EPIC EXPEDITION

Page 48

WATER WORLD

Page 49

FOODS OF THE WORLD

Page 50

SPEEDY SILHOUETTES

Page 51

A8	B5	C9	D11
E6	F2	G12	H7
I10	J1	K3	L4

TRUE OR FALSE?
Page 52

1. False	4. False	7. False	10. True
2. False	5. False	8. True	
3. True	6. True	9. True	

MATCHING PAIRS
Page 55

NUMBER PYRAMIDS
Page 57

PACKING JUMBLE
Page 58
There are 11 different items of clothing.

PAIR THEM UP
Page 59

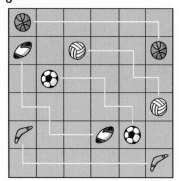

SPOT THE DIFFERENCE
Page 60

BIRD WATCH
Page 63
Six birds do not have a pair.

JIGSAW JUMBLE
Page 65
A theme park.

TOURIST TRIVIA
Page 66
The Sydney Opera House is in Australia.
The Statue of Liberty is in the United States of America.
Stonehenge is in the United Kingdom.
The Colosseum is in Italy.
The Eiffel Tower is in France.
The Pyramids of Giza are in Egypt.
The Parthenon is in Greece.
The Taj Mahal is in India.

PAIR THEM UP
Page 67

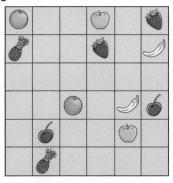

TIME-ZONE TRIVIA
Page 68

1. a) 24
2. b) Canada
3. a) They are on opposite sides of the Earth.
4. b) 9 am
5. 15:00 = Cairo
   8:00 = New York
   18:00 = Mumbai

PICTURE SUDOKU
Page 69

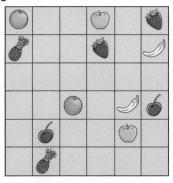

TREASURE TROVE FIX
Page 70

BALLOON CHAOS
Page 71
Aaron's balloon is about to fly away.

TRANSPORT SUDOKU
Page 72

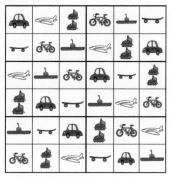

ODD ONE OUT
Page 73

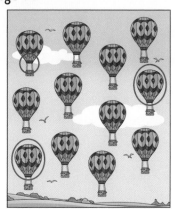

SAFARI SURPRISE
Page 74
A = elephants
B= giraffes
C = lions
D = rhinos

TRANSPORT WORDSEARCH
Page 75

PENGUIN PARADE
Page 77

MARKET MAYHEM
Page 79
Bicycles = 1
Red caps = 3
Birds = 6
Cats = 1
Guitars = 1
Vases for sale = 3
Sun umbrellas = 2
Rugs for sale = 3
Total = 20

PLAYGROUND PUZZLE
Page 82

ODD ONE OUT
Page 84

MAGIC MIRROR CHALLENGE
Page 85
1. c   2. a   3. b

DEEP-SEA DIVE
Page 86
Route C

SPOT THE DIFFERENCE
Page 88